Focus on Climate Change

CLIMATE CHANGE EFFECTS

How Our World Is Affected

REBECCA SCHROEDER

TWENTY-FIRST CENTURY BOOKS / MINNEAPOLIS

For everyone, everywhere, who was, is, or will be impacted by climate change.

Twenty-First Century Books™
An imprint of Lerner Publishing Group, Inc.
241 First Avenue North
Minneapolis, MN 55401 USA

For reading levels and more information, look up this title at www.lernerbooks.com.

Main body text set in Bembo Std Regular.
Typeface provided by Monotype Typography.

Library of Congress Cataloging-in-Publication Data

Names: Schroeder, Rebecca author
Title: Climate change effects : how our world is affected / Rebecca Schroeder.
Description: Minneapolis, MN : Twenty-First Century Books, [2026] | Series: Focus on climate change | Includes bibliographical references and index. | Audience: Ages 11–18 | Audience: Grades 7–9 | Summary: "Many people know what climate change is and impacts such as warming temperatures. But what other ways will climate change affect Earth and its inhabitants? Find out more about effects on everything from farming to migration"—Provided by publisher.
Identifiers: LCCN 2025010828 (print) | LCCN 2025010829 (ebook) | ISBN 9798765644225 library binding | ISBN 9798348029593 paperback | ISBN 9798348000141 epub
Subjects: LCSH: Climatic changes—Effect of human beings on—Juvenile literature | Climatic changes—Effect of agriculture on—Juvenile literature | Climatic changes—Economic aspects—Juvenile literature
Classification: LCC QC903.15 .S28 2026 (print) | LCC QC903.15 (ebook) | DDC 304.2/8—dc23/eng/20250609

LC record available at https://lccn.loc.gov/2025010828
LC ebook record available at https://lccn.loc.gov/2025010829

Manufactured in the United States of America
1-1012704-52448-5/2/2025

CONTENTS

INTRODUCTION

Water has always been both friend and foe to countries situated near bodies of water. In the twenty-first century, it has caused numerous disasters. For example, floods are a natural part of life in Bangladesh, home to the world's largest river delta and three powerful river systems. Farmers have learned to rely on predictable monsoon floods for growing crops such as rice that thrive in flooded soil. But in the 2010s, floods became more frequent, intense, deadly, and unpredictable due to climate change.

In 2017 severe flooding affected 3.9 million people in Bangladesh alone, also impacting India and Nepal. It was called the worst flooding in thirty years, despite previous cyclone-caused floods already claiming hundreds of thousands of lives. Then in 2020 unusually heavy monsoon rains left one-third of the country underwater. In 2022 more record-breaking floods hit, affecting an estimated 7.2 million people in Bangladesh. The aid organization International Federation of Red Cross and Red Crescent Societies called them "one of the worst floodings ever seen."

Fatikchhari, Chittagong, Bangladesh, faced more severe flooding in August 2024.

Increasing Disaster

Bangladesh has long faced floods, but the frequency of severe events in a short period is unusual. Once rare, extreme weather events such as these are becoming more common globally due to climate change. Climate change brings more frequent and severe storms, droughts, hurricanes, and wildfires—even in areas that haven't experienced them before.

Climate change is also evident in rising sea levels affecting coastal communities, crop losses due to droughts and floods, and melting glaciers leading to water scarcity. It affects ecosystems, species diversity, and human health. We'll discuss these effects and more in this book.

Melting glaciers are a telltale sign that climate change is making the planet warmer.

CHAPTER ONE
A Changing Climate

Before examining what climate change is and how it happens, it's important to define climate. People often confuse climate with weather. Weather refers to short-term atmospheric conditions, while climate is the average long-term weather for a region. For example, if you see rain outside, that's weather. Weather changes daily or hourly. If you live in Bangladesh, you're familiar with the rainy monsoon season from June to October—that's the region's climate. In contrast, the Atacama Desert in Chile has an incredibly dry climate year-round and rarely gets rain.

Though climate and weather differ, climate change alters weather patterns. The general trend scientists expect to see is that wet areas will tend to get wetter, and dry areas will get drier. Severe weather, hurricanes, wildfires, and other natural disasters will become more frequent and intense, and occur in places previously unaffected. The start and length of seasons will also shift. For example, in some regions, spring will begin earlier. And both spring and summer will last longer than what was previously typical for those regions.

What Is Climate Change?

According to the National Aeronautics and Space Administration (NASA), "climate change is a long-term change in the average weather patterns that have come to define Earth's local, regional, and global climates." Having these changes be long-term, not temporary, is key. Natural factors, including volcanic eruptions and solar events, can cause temporary climate change, but human activity has been the sole cause of long-term change since the eighteenth century.

Beginning with the Industrial Revolution (1733–1913), humans have produced increasing amounts of greenhouse

The Fagradalsfjall volcano erupts on the Reykjanes Peninsula in Iceland. Volcanic eruptions can cause short-term climate change.

gases, especially carbon dioxide (CO_2) and methane. These gases thicken Earth's atmosphere and trap heat as a blanket would. As a result, the global average temperature has increased by nearly 2°F (1.1°C) since the start of the Industrial Revolution. This seemingly small change has already had a significant worldwide impact. Even slight changes affect all Earth's interconnected systems—oceans, atmosphere, ice caps, and landmasses.

Climate Models

Scientists track climate change using computer simulations called climate models. These models assess possible climate change impacts and their severity, accounting for various factors that influence Earth's climate. Advanced computer programs calculate how changes in one factor affect the overall climate. Additionally, scientists use climate models to test different average global temperatures and predict environmental consequences.

Climate scientists constantly refine these models for accuracy. They validate their models using hindcasting, which deduces past events instead of predicting future ones. Paleoclimatologists, scientists who study ancient climates, play a key role by analyzing fossilized plants, tree rings, and ice cores for past climate clues. Satellite data also provides insights into past climates and weather patterns. During hindcasting, climate scientists can plug in factors to create models of ancient climates. Then, by comparing those model predictions to known past climates, they gain confidence in their accuracy for future predictions. But what are those predictions?

Paleoclimatologists study plant fossils and other indicators to learn about ancient climates.

Droughts, Rainfall, and Climate Change

Rising global temperatures will cause wet climates to become even wetter because warm air can hold more moisture than cold air. In fact, for every 1.8°F (1°C) that air temperature increases, it can hold about 7 percent more water vapor. These changes will become more drastic as Earth's average temperature rises. Water evaporates faster at higher temperatures. Warmer air and oceans increase evaporation.

Water vapor then cools and condenses into clouds. Eventually, the water droplets grow and fall as precipitation, such as rain, snow, or hail.

In short, warmer temperatures cause more evaporation and precipitation. This is why the Arctic and Antarctic are expected to become wetter due to climate change. Their cold temperatures limit air moisture. But as they warm, more precipitation will occur.

Hotter and Drier

Wet areas will become wetter, while dry areas will get drier. Rising global temperatures make the air hotter, leading to more evaporation. Even in deserts with scarce water, some amount of existing moisture in the soil evaporates. It's not enough to form rain clouds, but the heat dries out the soil and plants, intensifying and prolonging droughts.

Intense, persistent droughts are worsening wildfires worldwide. For example, in 2020 a drought affected many of the western and central areas of the United States. Combined with intense heat waves, the drought caused vegetation such as shrubs and trees to lose more moisture than normal. This made the vegetation more likely to catch fire, resulting in a positive feedback loop. In the loop, wildfires release stored carbon dioxide into the atmosphere. This traps more heat and causes even hotter temperatures, further intensifying droughts and wildfires. Though wildfires are common in parts of the United States and occur annually, the intense drought and heat brought on by the feedback loop resulted in a record amount of acres burned that year.

Water Availability

Some regions might not become wetter or drier overall. But climate change can still impact water availability and quality, leading to more issues. For example, warmer winters mean more precipitation falls as rain instead of snow, which is a problem for areas relying on snowpack for drinking water. Snowpack is snow that stays on the ground for months, slowly melting and providing meltwater during warmer seasons—a vital water source for millions of people.

Reduced snowfall also triggers a positive feedback loop. Hotter temperatures lead to less snow, which then contributes to even hotter temperatures. Lighter surfaces such as snow reflect sunlight, while darker ones, including forests, rocks, and soil, absorb it. Less snow means more heat absorption, further warming Earth.

Extreme Temperatures and Storms

Have you ever met someone who thinks cold weather disproves climate change? Since climate change involves an overall increase in global temperatures, people often refer to it as global warming. But this term can be misleading. Some assume it means every place on Earth is warming all the time, which isn't true.

On average, the 2010s was the hottest decade in recorded history. In the 2020s, high-temperature records are being set more often than low ones. Winters are generally warmer than in the past, but extreme cold still occurs. In the US, the early 2020s saw spikes of extremely cold air, severe ice storms, and

350.org

The global organization 350.org is fighting for "a world beyond fossil fuels." They promote renewable energy and people-powered campaigns all around the world. Often, the people who contribute the least to climate change suffer the worst of its effects. The organization collaborates with these communities to work toward a more sustainable and just future. They offer courses, training, and toolkits online for people of all ages who'd like to engage with climate change issues.

The organization's name refers to 350 parts per million. This is the concentration of carbon dioxide compared to other molecules in the atmosphere that is considered "safe." That is, it would ensure a future that avoids the most significant impacts of climate change. The actual concentration of carbon dioxide in the atmosphere changes yearly and has been climbing as greenhouse gas emissions increase. The world surpassed the concentration of 350 parts per million in the late 1980s, and 350.org is hoping to inspire people to help lower it and reach a safe concentration.

As total greenhouse gas emissions go up, so does the concentration of CO_2 in the atmosphere.

heavy snowfall in unexpected places. These events are linked to the polar vortex.

The polar vortex is a large region with cold air and low pressure that surrounds the North Pole. Scientists are studying how Arctic warming affects atmospheric patterns. One theory suggests that shrinking temperature differences between freezing polar areas and warmer southern regions make the polar jet stream, a belt of wind in the atmosphere, less stable, causing the polar vortex to stretch southward. This brings cold temperatures and turns rain into snow or ice. So, despite global warming, climate change can still worsen winters.

Hot and cold temperatures aren't the only things pushed to extremes by climate change. Extreme precipitation events are when the amount of rain or snow that falls is much higher than normal for a region. In the United States, the average number of days per year with extreme precipitation events remained mostly constant throughout most of the 1900s. But "nine of the top 10 years for extreme one-day precipitation events have occurred since 1996," says the US Environmental Protection Agency.

Climate change is causing stronger storms too. For example, warmer air and warmer ocean temperatures lead to increased wind speed in tropical storms, including hurricanes and cyclones. Scientists measure hurricanes and cyclones using a five-step scale, the Saffir–Simpson scale. A Category 5 storm is one with winds of sustained speeds above 157 miles (253 km) per hour. These wind speeds are incredibly destructive to property, nature, and any people or animals in their path. But within the last decade, five hurricanes have had sustained winds faster than 192 miles (309 km) per hour.

This sets them apart as a new breed of storms capable of even more destruction. Some scientists say this means a new step on the scale is necessary—a Category 6 storm.

Climate and Ocean Currents

Warmer ocean water that comes with climate change also affects ocean currents. Ocean currents heavily influence the climate in different areas of the world. If the currents change, then even more climate change will happen.

The global ocean conveyor belt is a system of water that moves constantly. Temperature and the amount of salt in the

Surface ocean currents take warm water to Earth's poles, increasing glacier melting.

water impact its behavior. The water in the conveyor belt includes surface currents that carry warm ocean water from the equator to the poles. And its currents in the deep ocean carry denser, colder, saltier water in the opposite direction.

A warming climate means warmer oceans. This is due to a higher average global temperature, as well as more glaciers and sea ice melting. Warming oceans—and more freshwater making its way into the ocean from melting glaciers on land—will disrupt the sinking of the coldest, densest, saltiest water. This could slow down the global ocean conveyor belt. These currents are the reason why temperatures are so mild in Europe, even though the continent is quite far north from the equator. If these currents were to weaken, temperatures in Europe would become colder.

As we've seen so far, climate change can significantly alter an area's temperature and amount of precipitation. These can both greatly impact the weather a region experiences, especially severe storms and natural disasters. Climate change can make winters colder and snowier, while making summers hotter. It can cause dry areas to become even drier, increasing the possibility of wildfires. And it can cause waterlogged areas to experience even more precipitation, resulting in floods or landslides. Even a slight change in temperature or precipitation can have devastating effects on the region's agriculture too, including the food and water supply of its inhabitants.

CHAPTER TWO

Food, Water, and Agriculture

Shrinking snowpack is an issue for areas that rely on melted snow for drinking water. But meltwater can come from the melting of glaciers as well. Glaciers cover around 10 percent of Earth's surface. They're one of the major places on the globe where freshwater is stored. High mountain regions are home to about 10 percent of the world's population, and melting glaciers will affect the lives of those people in many ways.

But it's not just the people in the mountains who are affected. A staggering 1.9 billion people live downstream of glaciers or snowpacks. They depend on annual meltwater for drinking, hydroelectric power, and irrigation. Worsening glacial melt is such a pressing issue that the United Nations General Assembly declared 2025 the International Year of Glaciers' Preservation.

The Shrinking Glaciers of the Andes

The Andes mountains, a range in western South America, are ground zero for melting glaciers. Most of this loss is

In Utah, 95 percent of the population, such as the citizens of Salt Lake City, relies on water from snowpack runoff.

concentrated in the ice fields of Patagonia in the southern tip of South America. These glaciers often melt faster than the others in the mountain range because they lie at lower altitudes, or nearer sea level. This makes them more vulnerable to rising temperatures because temperatures are already higher at lower altitudes. The air is denser nearer the ground or sea, meaning it can absorb and hold more heat.

Glaciers in the Andes aren't only a source of drinking water for millions of people, but they are also culturally and spiritually significant. Mountains and the glaciers atop them are sacred to many of the Indigenous peoples in the region. In Peru, the country with the most glaciers in South America, people make spiritual pilgrimages to some of the glaciers and bring offerings to the ice. Traditionally, they'd also cut blocks of ice from the glacier to bring home with them. But by 2012 the pilgrims had noticed that the glaciers were smaller than normal. They no longer cut pieces of them in hopes that the glaciers will stop dwindling.

Scientists who have studied these glaciers in the field and via satellite are able to put numbers to the shrinking. Across the Andes, 98 percent of glaciers shrunk between 1900 and 2020. From just 2000 to 2016, glaciers in Peru shrunk by nearly a third and, from 2000 to 2020, became 3 feet (0.9 m) thinner each year. And between the 1980s and 2020, the region as a whole lost between 30 and 50 percent of its ice cover.

These shrinking glaciers affect the Andean region in several ways. Water shortages impact communities that depend on glacial melt for their drinking water. They also reduce the amount of electricity that comes from hydroelectric power plants. Glacial melt from the region supplies water to many rivers in the Amazon Basin—home of the world's largest rainforest. So, impacts reach beyond the mountains into neighboring areas.

Rural farmers and major cities are among the most affected. Major population centers—including Quito, Ecuador, and La Paz, Bolivia—depend on meltwater from glaciers. In Quito, meltwater makes up 5 percent of the city's water supply most years and up to 15 percent in a drought year. In La Paz, glacial melt makes up 61 percent of the water supply and up to 85 percent in a drought year. With glaciers shrinking, the region faces a water shortage. Farmers rely on water for irrigation. When the water supply dwindles, farmers must find a new livelihood or switch to crops that require less water to grow.

The Melting of the Third Pole

While the Andes may be the site of the most significant glacial melting relative to the region's size, the Himalayan mountains in Asia are the region where the most people will suffer the most widespread impacts. The Himalayas are often called the world's Third Pole. After the North Pole and the South Pole, the region contains the most glaciers in the world.

In the Indus Basin alone—which includes Afghanistan, China, India, and Pakistan—206 million people source their water from high-altitude lakes and glaciers. This area's population is expected to increase dramatically during the twenty-first century, putting further strain on water supplies. In the same time frame, the region's average temperature is expected to increase by about 3.5°F (1.9°C). This increase will make the climate's dry season worse and increase water demand even more.

There are even more people who face these water risks than just those in the basin. Around two billion people live downstream of rivers that begin in the Himalayas. Water flowing into this region—including into some of the world's most famous rivers, such as the Indus, Mekong, and Ganges—is projected to peak around 2050. This means that after 2050, the water supply in this region will dwindle. If climate change remains unchecked, glaciers in the Himalayan region are expected to lose 75 percent of their ice between the 2020s and 2100.

Populations in these downstream regions will experience the opposing impacts of too much water and yet not enough. Glaciers do not melt at a steady pace, so much of the increased glacial melt will cause flooding and trigger landslides around these mighty rivers. This will displace people who live along the banks. Scientists have also noted that depressions left behind when glaciers receded during the last ice age have been filling with water due to excessive glacial melt. They form glacial lakes, which bring a significant risk of outburst flooding—a type of flooding where the land or ice around lakes becomes too weak to contain the water. Such effects are already happening, as both floods and avalanches in the region have increased between the 2010s and 2020s.

The mighty Ganges River flows out of the Himalayan mountains, providing water for hundreds of millions of people on its way to the ocean.

At the same time, permanent glacier loss will eventually result in water shortages in the region, affecting the availability of water for drinking, agriculture, and hydroelectricity. For example, countries such as Nepal—which gets most of its electricity from hydroelectric power—could experience large setbacks if the flow of water is interrupted or lessened.

Agriculture and Food Supply

As glaciers shrink, irrigation for agriculture will become less reliable in regions dependent on meltwater. Changing weather patterns, especially factors such as higher temperatures, increased droughts, and more precipitation, will make it harder to grow crops in certain areas. As climates change, some crops that were once well-suited for the temperature and rainfall in an area might become difficult to grow in the new conditions. Some areas that were once too dry to farm may become fertile land, while other areas where crops once flourished may now be too dry to grow them.

The more specific impacts on agriculture vary from region to region and crop to crop. For example, the greenhouse gas carbon dioxide is one contributor to climate change. But it is also necessary for photosynthesis and the storage of water in plants. Higher temperatures could make the plants grow faster. This may seem like a positive impact on plants. But when plants such as wheat grow too fast, they produce less grain. Farmers get less output from seeds, and the overall food supply decreases.

A 2021 study by NASA indicated that production of corn could decrease by 24 percent globally by 2030. Corn is grown

Permaculture and Regenerative Agriculture

Farmers and scientists are working to make agriculture more sustainable and healthier for the planet. Permaculture is a type of agriculture that aims for sustainable, self-sufficient systems that don't produce any waste. It's an approach to the management of land and resources that tries to mimic the interconnected parts of natural ecosystems. Permaculture advocates for growing many different crops together and rotating them in ways that benefit the soil and the crops themselves. Examples of permaculture methods include creating an "agroforest" where fruits, vegetables, and trees all grow together and collecting rainwater to use for plumbing, watering plants, and more.

Unlike permaculture, regenerative agriculture focuses mainly on food production with the goal of restoring soil and ecosystem health. Practices include feeding and preserving microbes (organisms such as bacteria that are microscopic or smaller) in the ground to promote healthy soil and limiting the use of chemical weed or bug killers.

Farmers who practice regenerative agriculture focus on techniques that preserve the fertility of the soil.

in countries near the equator. Rising temperatures there will have an adverse effect on crop yields. But other crops, such as wheat, may end up seeing a growth in production. This is because changes in temperature and rainfall caused by climate change could make it possible to grow wheat in places that haven't historically been suited for it. So, while wheat might put out less grain, it might also grow in more places.

Natural disasters that are made more common by climate change will also affect crop yield. For example, drier and warmer regions will experience a greater risk of wildfires, which can destroy farmers' fields. If dry land becomes drier due to changes in climate or human activities such as deforestation (a process called desertification), this will also cause issues. Nearly half of the world's agricultural land is classified as drylands. Studies show that human-caused climate change has already degraded 12.6 percent of these lands and driven them toward desertification. When this once-fertile land becomes a desert, it can no longer sustain agriculture.

The opposite end of the spectrum is also dangerous. In regions that receive more precipitation than normal, climate change could cause soil erosion. Soil erosion is the loosening or washing away of the top layer of soil. This can make it harder for plants to take hold and decrease the nutrients in the soil since the top layer is where most nutrients are found. Since the top layer of soil also contains agricultural chemicals such as pesticides, soil erosion can harm the water quality of nearby lakes, rivers, and streams.

The impacts of climate change on agriculture can seem scary. People need the food that agriculture provides to survive. One positive sign is that agricultural scientists are

Scientists continue to work on making crops hardier, such as breeding a type of corn that can thrive in dry conditions.

already working on breeding crops that are more resistant to the stresses that come with climate change. In fact, a type of drought-resistant corn that was introduced in 2011 accounted for nearly a fourth of all corn planted just five years later. Farmers recognize the need to adapt their practices to the new normal of a changed climate.

Plants, Pests, and Pollinators

In general, higher temperatures mean that northern regions will see extended growing seasons and more days without frost on the ground. Though this can increase the volume of crops produced, it will also require more water for irrigation. Additionally, changing temperatures and precipitation will affect when crops bloom and when pollinators such as bees and butterflies emerge. In the United States, pollination, which often occurs when pollinators carry pollen between plants, is imperative for hundreds of plants to reproduce. If pollinators emerge at a different time than when plants bloom, it could affect the life cycle of many crops.

Higher temperatures also mean that as crops can be grown in new areas, pests will extend their range to different regions. Studies also show that climate change can "promote and expand pesticide resistance" in insects. This can make pests more common and endanger the crops they attack or feed on.

Pests will also become more common because higher temperatures cause changes in their life cycles. A study from the University of California illustrated this by examining populations of three major pests that attack walnut, peach, and almond crops in the state. The study revealed that warmer temperatures could cause the pests to appear nearly a month earlier than usual in the springtime. It also predicted that the time between pest generations will shorten. More generations of these pests appearing within the same growing season can cause more crop destruction and increase the need for pesticides. This comes with high financial costs and can harm beneficial insects in the ecosystem.

The multiplication of pests and the diseases they carry isn't the only threat climate change brings to humans. Communities face all kinds of risks, from rising sea levels to air quality concerns to economic impacts.

CHAPTER THREE

Human Health and Communities

Climate change doesn't just affect landscapes. People may also experience negative consequences. Rising sea levels, for example, are a threat to people and entire communities that occupy coastlines and nearby low-lying areas. Changes in climate may cause people to lose their livelihoods and their homes, affecting them financially. Climate change, along with more intense and more frequent natural disasters, can have serious consequences for human health.

Rising Sea Levels

Wetlands protect coastal communities. Wetlands are regions that are completely covered with or saturated by water, such as swamps and marshes. They store carbon dioxide, preventing it from escaping into the atmosphere and worsening the effects of climate change. Coastal wetlands serve as an important buffer zone to minimize damage during hurricanes, which, as we discussed in chapter one, are becoming more intense. But sea level rise is causing these important coastal ecosystems to disappear. One example of this is occurring in Louisiana. As of 2016, the state has lost more than 2,000 square miles (5,180 sq. km) of land (mostly wetlands) due to rising seas since 1932.

Rising sea levels affect more than just wetlands. More than one-third of the world's population lives within about 62 miles (100 km) of a coastline. In the United States, around 42 percent of the population lives in a coastal county. Development due to tourism and business has caused severe erosion of beaches and the destruction of coastal habitats in these regions. Climate change will only make these problems worse.

Threatened by rising sea levels, residents of the port city of Rotterdam in the Netherlands have been building floating houses.

Increased rainfall and coastal erosion have also caused floods to occur much more frequently. Around the world, fourteen million people living in coastal communities face a 5 percent chance of flooding each year. Scientific models predict that if the rate of climate change faced in the 2020s continues, that number will increase to seventy-three million people by 2100.

Places in Peril

Many highly populated cities and important ports occupy coastal regions worldwide. This means that floods and rising sea levels will have a widespread human and economic impact. Scientists have outlined a "worst-case warming scenario" involving an average global temperature rise of at least 8°F (5°C) by 2100. In late 2023 climate models predicted that by the end of the century, if this scenario were to become reality, major population centers including Kolkata, India; Rio de Janeiro, Brazil; Guayaquil, Ecuador; and Sydney, Australia, would have more than 5 percent of city land below sea level . . . permanently.

Severe consequences aren't limited to only the worst-case scenarios of cities. Even if the world cuts its greenhouse gas emissions in half from 2021 levels by 2050, entire low-lying countries are still at risk. The Cayman Islands, Maldives, Marshall Islands, Netherlands, Saint Martin, Turks and Caicos, and Tuvalu are projected to end up with at least 5 percent of their territory permanently submerged due to rising sea levels.

The Maldives face particular risks. It is a remote nation consisting of more than 1,200 separate islands. Four-

The low-lying islands of the Maldives are projected to be mostly underwater by 2100.

fifths of them lie no more than around 3 feet (1 m) above sea level. The country's capital city, Malé, sits at about 6 feet (2 m) above sea level. The country has already built a 10-foot (3-m) high sea wall around Malé. But much of the nation is expected to be underwater by 2100. To draw awareness to the pressing issue of how rising sea levels due to climate change will affect the country, the former president of the Maldives hosted an underwater cabinet meeting in 2009 with politicians clad in scuba gear. Since then, the Maldives has continued to push for stronger international climate agreements, and its leaders have focused on funding projects to make their country more resilient to climate change.

Kiribati: A Case Study

Kiribati is another one of the lowest-lying island nations worldwide. This small Pacific nation is one of the lowest-income countries in the world and one of the lowest contributors to greenhouse gas emissions. Despite its insignificant contribution to climate change, Kiribati is one of the countries whose people will suffer the most from its consequences.

Kiribati is a collection of thirty-three atolls. On average, they are less than 7 feet (2 m) above sea level. Rising tides have already submerged two of them. King tides, which are particularly high tides, used to affect the country once or twice a year. But they've become more intense and occur more often. The frequent flooding from these tides has contaminated freshwater ponds with saltwater. It has also harmed crops.

People in Kiribati have already begun to migrate inland to escape the flooding. But that is only a temporary solution. Looking ahead to a time when more of the country's approximately 121,000 citizens will be displaced, in 2014 the nation's government purchased land in Fiji. Citizens will be able to go there once the sea level gets too high. Residents may last until the waves are literally at their doorsteps, but chances are that they'll be forced to leave before the islands are fully submerged. Predictions suggest that by 2050, over half of Kiribati's most populated island will be vulnerable to storm surges. Rising sea levels and flooding from storm surges can contaminate farmland and underground fresh water supplies. So even if their houses still stand above the tide, people may be forced to leave due to a lack of food and water.

The Climate Refugees of Kiribati

The term *refugee* is often used to describe people who must leave their homes due to war or a similar crisis. Communities and countries worldwide have taken steps to help the people who are or will be forced from their homes due to climate change. In 2013 Kiribati resident Ioane Teitiota applied for protection as a refugee in New Zealand. He argued that his life was at risk due to how the rising sea levels were affecting his home in Kiribati. His island was once home to less than two thousand residents. But the population ballooned to more than fifty thousand due to other places in the country becoming uninhabitable. Teitiota argued that since the island was predicted to be completely uninhabitable within the next fifteen years, making him return would put his life in danger.

New Zealand ended up rejecting Teitiota's claim and refugee application, stating that his life was not in immediate danger and sending him back to Kiribati. The United Nations Human Rights Committee agreed with the court's ruling. This was a defeat for Teitiota and his family. But the court case caused the United Nations to assert that "it is unlawful for governments to return people to countries where their lives might be threatened by the climate crisis." While they did not find Teitiota's life to be sufficiently threatened, they've left the door open to help others in the future who must flee their homes because of climate change.

The government of Kiribati is helping ensure that its people will be safe in the future. Aside from buying land in Fiji, the government is helping workers develop skills that can give them a chance to get jobs overseas. While keeping people safe is crucial, lives will not be the only thing lost if the sea swallows Kiribati. If entire nations are forced to migrate, there will be a vast loss of cultural resources. Cultural heritage sites will be left behind, and even destroyed, and ancestral lands will be lost. It will be hard to avoid the loss of language and traditions as residents of low-lying island nations are forced to seek shelter within the borders of other countries that do not speak the same language or practice the same traditions. The island nations that face the risk of cultural destruction are not alone in their plight. By the year 2050, sea level rise is expected to threaten around 191 of 284 important cultural heritage sites in Africa.

Meeting at their parliament buildings, the Kiribati government decided to buy land in Fiji in preparation for the need to migrate because of climate change.

Climate Refugees

Climate Refugees is a nonprofit organization that advocates for the rights of people displaced by climate change. The organization's goal is to help protect climate refugees and generate global awareness of their plight. Part of their work includes supporting the creation of legal policies that would protect people displaced by climate change or who need to migrate to avoid the impacts of climate change. Another major focus of the organization is telling the stories of displaced people. On the organization's website, you can find videos where people directly impacted by climate change are interviewed and tell their stories.

Climate Change and Health Issues

Rising sea levels aren't the only way that climate change puts lives at risk. It might seem odd that climate change can cause health issues. But remember that climate change intensifies a lot of natural disasters and causes the habitats of disease-spreading pests to expand. Natural disasters bring with them a host of health issues. Water-borne diseases spread during floods, and respiratory illnesses arise from wildfire smoke. Many of the health issues caused by climate change already exist. They're becoming more widespread and occurring more frequently and intensely.

Additionally, droughts and higher temperatures will result in more heat-related illnesses. Already, research has found that 37 percent of deaths due to heat-related issues can be linked to human-caused climate change. Warmer weather also provides better growing conditions for microbes, some of which can make people and animals sick.

Worldwide, hundreds of millions of people face hunger. Destruction of crops due to floods, droughts, or natural disasters can make malnutrition and starvation even more common. Worse and more frequent natural disasters can impact health care facilities and the distribution of medical supplies, especially to communities with less infrastructure. The World Health Organization predicts that "between 2030 and 2050, climate change is expected to cause approximately 250,000 additional deaths per year from undernutrition, malaria, diarrhea, and heat stress alone."

As populations are forced to migrate due to climate change, their health can suffer as well. In addition to putting one's physical health at risk, having to leave one's home or experiencing traumatic natural disasters can cause mental health concerns, such as the development of post-traumatic stress disorder—a disorder caused by a highly stressful event that is often marked by depression, anxiety, nightmares, and other effects.

Climate Change and Air Quality

Air pollution is another existing issue that climate change will worsen. Ozone is a type of gas made of three oxygen atoms bonded together. It's formed when heat and sunlight cause chemical reactions involving nitrogen oxide gases. Ozone is beneficial higher up in Earth's atmosphere (specifically in the stratosphere) because it forms the ozone layer, which blocks most of the sun's harmful ultraviolet radiation from reaching

Earth's surface. But ground-level ozone is associated with smog (a fog made of smoke and chemical fumes) and harms human health. According to the Centers for Disease Control and Prevention, both ground-level ozone and particulate matter—microscopic solids that are so small they can be inhaled and cause serious health problems—lead to lowered lung function, early death, and increased hospital visits due to asthma. Climate change is expected to increase both these air pollutants, with ground-level ozone levels expected to increase due to hotter temperatures and higher methane levels.

Similarly, warmer temperatures will cause allergy seasons to lengthen. Summers will be hotter and longer, and spring will start sooner. Allergy symptoms will worsen due to greater amounts of pollen. This will affect people with other respiratory issues too. When people with asthma, for

Smog, which causes poor air quality and greater health risks, hangs over the city of Mumbai, India.

example, are exposed to allergens such as pollen, it increases the chance they'll have an asthma attack and need to be admitted to the hospital. Additionally, when paired with higher amounts of rainfall, warmer temperatures can also cause more mold to grow indoors. More mold will also cause people to experience respiratory issues more often.

Economic Impact of Climate Change

The entire world is feeling the effects of climate change. But it is often the lowest-income nations that are the most affected. Such countries, such as Bangladesh or Kiribati, often haven't done much to contribute to climate change. But they generally experience more of its negative effects than wealthier countries whose actions have largely been to blame.

Most of the world's lowest-income countries—and therefore the world's lowest-income people—are in South Asia and Sub-Saharan Africa. Both regions are projected to be greatly affected by climate change. These are also some of the hottest places on Earth, which makes adapting to climate change and rising temperatures more difficult because people there are already struggling to stay cool in soaring temperatures. Additionally, many of these countries have fewer funds and technologies available to help them adapt to the effects of climate change. The world's lowest-income people also tend to depend economically on farming, forestry, and fishing—all sectors that climate change will heavily impact. These people may not have access to adequate health care either, which is necessary to help them recover from the health effects of climate change or natural disasters.

As we've discussed, climate change can negatively affect human health, cause worse and more frequent natural disasters, disrupt agriculture, and make water less available. All these consequences will be particularly hard for people already suffering from poverty who may already face these challenges or not have adequate resources to combat them. These impacts will also push more people into poverty, as impacts of climate change often include higher food prices, deteriorating health conditions, and exposure to disasters. In fact, the World Bank estimates that "climate change will drive between 68 million and 135 million people into poverty by 2030."

Climate Culprits

It's no secret that the largest contributors to climate change have historically been the wealthiest nations in the world. The richest countries produce nearly 40 percent of carbon dioxide emissions despite only hosting 16 percent of the world's population. Conversely, the lowest-income countries on Earth—which make up more than half of the world's population—account for less than 15 percent of emissions. Rich countries, such as the United States, China, Germany, the United Kingdom, and Japan, experienced the most benefits of the Industrial Revolution while producing more than their fair share of greenhouse gas emissions. This means these countries and their citizens both produce more emissions and are better suited to adapt to the consequences.

In response to this, many people are calling for those nations responsible for emitting the most greenhouse gases throughout history to provide aid to less industrialized

Major power plants, such as this coal-fired one in Arizona, are one way wealthy countries such as the United States contribute to greenhouse gas emissions.

countries facing more severe impacts. Another way for major emitters to take responsibility would be for these countries to set models for their peers by enacting stronger environmental policies and taking the most ambitious actions when it comes to preventing climate change. Potential actions such as these are central to the idea of environmental justice.

Environmental Justice

The term *environmental justice* originated in the 1980s. It includes working toward the equitable distribution of environmental benefits and harms, and the involvement of all people in decisions that affect health and the environment. In the United States, the environmental justice movement initially centered around the fact that landfills were most often located near low-income communities of people of color. These communities experienced more pollution and other risks, which are forms of environmental injustice. When applied to the issue of climate change, environmental justice is also often called climate equity.

The fact that climate change affects lower-income countries with fewer resources most is an environmental justice issue. The goal of environmental justice is for everyone on the planet to have access to a healthy environment, decision-making power, and the same amount of protection from health and environmental hazards. Environmental justice calls for extra support for communities facing the most impacts from climate change and those with existing challenges (such as poverty or widespread health concerns) that climate change will worsen.

But humans aren't the only species whose communities and health are at risk due to climate change. Changing temperatures will affect the health of everything on the planet—from ocean dwellers to entire ecosystems.

CHAPTER FOUR
Oceans and Ecosystems

We've discussed some impacts that climate change will have on oceans. Ice will melt, currents will change, and seas will rise. But there are some equally important but less obvious impacts on oceans that climate change will cause.

Ocean Acidification

As its name suggests, ocean acidification means that the world's oceans are becoming more acidic over time. Oceans are a major carbon sink. This means that they excel at absorbing and storing carbon dioxide. In fact, oceans absorb about one-third of all human-made carbon dioxide. At first glance, this seems beneficial. After all, if the oceans are taking in carbon dioxide, a greenhouse gas, then less carbon dioxide is making its way into the atmosphere to cause even more global warming. But when oceans absorb carbon dioxide from the atmosphere, the gas dissolves and then reacts with the water molecules present to form carbonic acid.

This reaction releases hydrogen ions into the water. The more hydrogen ions there are, the lower the pH (a measure of how acidic or basic something is) and the more acidic something is.

One of the most immediate consequences of acidification is that the extra hydrogen ions in the ocean will tend to bond (when atoms or ions join together) with carbonate ions. Clams, crabs, corals, and mussels all have shells made of a compound called calcium carbonate. Calcium carbonate forms when calcium bonds with carbonate ions. So, those animals need carbonate ions to form their shells. When carbonate ions bond with hydrogen ions instead, populations of these animals are harmed. A decrease in the populations

Mussels are one animal that ocean acidification greatly impacts.

of these animals affects the whole food chain because some fish eat clams, crabs, mussels, and even coral. Plus, many fish depend on coral for shelter from predators and a safe place to lay their eggs. So, populations of fish will decrease, too. The people who depend on fish, crabs, clams, or mussels for food or economic gain will also be impacted.

Additionally, warmer temperatures caused by climate change actually reduce the ocean's ability to absorb carbon dioxide. Oceans absorb carbon dioxide at their surface. Then they rely on winds to mix surface waters with deeper waters. This allows the carbon dioxide to reach deeper parts of the ocean. Warmer temperatures make it harder for winds to mix the layers because the now warmer water is concentrated on the surface. This causes a much greater difference in density between the hotter surface water and the cooler, deeper water. With a greater difference in density, the mixing process is harder and takes longer. This slowdown causes the surface layer to reach the maximum amount of carbon dioxide it can hold because it can no longer pass some off to lower layers of the ocean.

Effects on Coral Reefs and Turtles

The combination of warmer and more acidic waters spells trouble for coral reefs. Coral reefs have a mutually beneficial relationship with the algae that live in them. The corals provide a safe home for the algae, and both species supply each other with nutrients that they need to live. When water temperatures get too hot, corals get stressed and kick these algae out. This is known as coral bleaching. Without algae and its nutrients, the coral turns completely white. Once bleached, corals are more vulnerable to disease. To recover from coral bleaching, corals need calcium carbonate. But as we mentioned earlier, ocean acidification causes supplies of this compound to dwindle.

Corals are so sensitive to warmer oceans that the Intergovernmental Panel on Climate Change (IPCC) predicts that a global average temperature rise of 3.6°F (2°C) from pre-industrial levels will cause 99 percent of warm-water coral reefs to disappear. Already, the Endangered Species Act lists twenty-five species of coral as endangered. This reef loss would negatively affect ocean life since corals support around one-fourth of marine creatures.

Warmer waters can also affect reptile populations by skewing the male-to-female ratio in the species. Reptiles such as turtles, alligators, and crocodiles all experience temperature-dependent sex determination. For example, turtle eggs maintained at warmer temperatures will develop

Rising ocean temperatures have caused coral bleaching in many oceans.

into female turtles. Scientists have found that warmer sand surrounding turtle nests will produce the same result. At colder temperatures, eggs will develop into male turtles. Nests that vary between warm and cold temperatures will result in a mix of female and male turtles.

Why does this matter? For a species to survive, it needs enough males and females to produce offspring. Climate change will make waters warmer, which will tip the scales toward the production of female baby turtles. Scientists are already seeing this happen. A 2020 study of green sea turtles in the northern Great Barrier Reef showed that almost all young turtles were female. Another study conducted in Florida between 2018 and 2022 saw the same result. Too many females and not enough males could lead to fewer offspring and decreased turtle populations.

Effects on Land Ecosystems

Climate change isn't only wreaking havoc on ocean life and systems. It is also drastically changing land ecosystems. Climate models have predicted that by 2100, more than 40 percent of ecosystems will transform. For example, dry shrubland could turn to desert, or frozen tundra could turn into boreal forests, the type of cold pine forests found in Canada. The ranges of certain pests are expanding due to warmer temperatures. The same is true for plants. Plants from a certain area are adapted to live in that climate. As climates change, plants must migrate too, but it takes place over multiple generations. For many plants, this means it could take place over several years. But for some types of trees, multiple generations means hundreds of years.

The Coral Restoration Foundation

The Coral Restoration Foundation's mission is to restore coral reefs and educate people on the importance of Earth's oceans. The foundation supports research regarding coral reef monitoring techniques and the natural recovery process of reefs. Much like gardeners growing plants in nurseries, the Coral Restoration Foundation grows genetically diverse, critically endangered corals in offshore nurseries. Then, it transplants them into select sites around the Florida Keys, a string of islands off the coast of Florida. If you ever go diving in the Florida Keys, you can help the group with data collection by downloading their OkCoral smartphone app.

The Coral Restoration Foundation works to restore reefs such as this one off of the Florida Keys.

The moose population on Michigan's Isle Royale has thrived since warmer temperatures forced the island's wolves to head north.

In general, researchers predict that biomes will shift toward Earth's poles. A biome, also known as a major life zone, is an area that includes naturally occurring communities of plants and animals that share common traits specific to that area, such as greater resistance to heat or cold. As biomes shift, the species that occupy them will have to adapt. Some species will be better than others at adapting. This means that some species will see their populations grow while others will see their populations shrink and possibly become extinct. The overall balance of ecosystems will be disrupted, and the biodiversity (biological variety of plants and animals in a region) of regions will be affected. An example of this can already be seen on Isle Royale in Lake Superior, north of Michigan's Upper Peninsula. Warmer weather has made it more difficult for wolves to survive, which has led to the moose population, part of the wolves' food source, becoming more abundant.

CHAPTER FIVE

Looking Toward the Future

In this book, we've discussed a variety of climate change impacts. But you might still be wondering, "How bad will it really get?" Scientists at the IPCC agree that if the average global temperature doesn't increase by more than 2.7°F (1.5°C) from the pre-industrial average by the year 2100, we will avoid the worst impacts. But achieving this would require immediate and forceful action from governments around the world. To achieve this, the global net carbon dioxide emissions would have to be zero by 2050, meaning the amount of emissions created and the amount removed from the atmosphere would be the same. Some action on avoiding climate change impacts has begun since many governments have come together under the 2016 Paris Agreement. This international agreement aims to limit global temperature rise to 3.6°F (2°C) from the pre-industrial average by the end of the century. This is less forceful of a measure than scientists have suggested, but it's a step in the right direction.

Climate models studied by IPCC scientists have found that as of 2023, "current global policies . . . would lead to a median warming of 3.2°C [5.76°F] by 2100." As mentioned earlier, the worst-case scenario involves an increase in greenhouse gas emissions, leading to an average global temperature rise of at least 8°F (5°C) by 2100. In this scenario, hundreds of millions of people across the world would become climate refugees. This includes a projected thirteen million people from Bangladesh alone. Large amounts of land in countries such as Vietnam and states such as Florida would disappear under rising seas. Cities including New Delhi, India, would experience an average temperature

Climate change could cause long stretches of dangerously high temperatures in places such as New Delhi, India. This increases the risk of heat stroke, dehydration, and respiratory problems.

close to 90°F (32°C) for around eight months of the year. How can the worst-case scenario be avoided?

Mitigation and Adaptation

Two strategies to tackle the impacts of climate change are mitigation and adaptation. Mitigation means dealing with the root cause, which is greenhouse gas emissions. Transitioning to renewable sources of energy such as wind and solar power; using public transportation, walking, or biking to limit or eliminate automobile emissions; making homes energy efficient; and planting trees are all strategies to help reduce greenhouse gases in the atmosphere. They will help lessen the impacts of climate change.

But even if warming is kept to 2.7°F (1.5°C) max, communities will still need to adapt to a changing climate. Adaptation means altering behaviors and systems to make communities more resilient to the impacts of climate change. What are some ways to adapt? People and communities can make sure they're ready for and know what to do in case of any type of natural disaster that might affect them. Coastal cities can build seawalls to keep the rising oceans at bay. Governments can update infrastructure such as roads, bridges, and public buildings to better withstand stronger storms and higher temperatures. Farmers can introduce more drought-resistant crop varieties and may have to change what they plant to adapt to changes in temperature.

Every community and country will have to adapt, but the United Nations estimates that the cost of adaptation could reach $300 billion annually for less industrialized countries. There are some ways people are working to help

Building seawalls to guard against rising ocean levels is an adaptation used in many coastal cities.

lower-income countries afford this heavy cost. Started in 2010, the global Adaptation Fund is one organization that finances projects to help communities in less-industrialized countries adapt to climate change. Governments and private donors fund it.

More Movements and Organizations

There are many citizen-driven organizations dedicated to environmental causes too. Some include climate advocacy, adaptation, or mitigation as a part of their mission. One example is the Climate Action Network, a global network that consists of more than 1,900 citizen-led organizations in over 130 countries. These organizations work under the network's umbrella to fight climate change and promote sustainability. The network also brings citizens to the annual United Nations climate negotiations and pushes governments to adopt national policies to combat climate change.

Some organizations are built around a specific community. For example, the Indigenous Environmental Network brings together Indigenous communities from around the world. They focus on protecting sacred sites and natural resources as well as promoting environmental justice. Another example is the Climate Collaborative. They focus on getting businesses in the grocery industry to take strong steps to reduce climate change. For example, Climate Collaborative runs a Commitment Program through which brands can commit to terms such as fully renewable power, reducing the climate impacts of packaging or transportation,

Reducing food waste is one of the many goals of Climate Collaborative's Commitment Program.

reducing food waste, or other goals. Over 265 food-related companies have already made at least one commitment.

Other organizations are built around a specific goal or idea involving climate change. One of these is the Biomimicry Institute. Biomimicry is a design strategy that aims to mimic nature. The institute leads the transfer of ideas and strategies from nature to promote sustainable industrial growth and ways to adapt to climate change. In a different vein, the Transition Network is geared toward change at the local and community level. The organization supports transition towns. These are communities working to become more resilient and reduce their carbon footprint.

CONCLUSION

Now Is the Time to Act

Climate change presents many challenges. It will affect every sphere of life—from food, farms, and water supply to oceans, cities, wildlife, and entire ecosystems. Temperatures will rise all around the globe. Natural disasters will be worse and more common. Human health will face new risks. People will be pushed into poverty. The populations of entire countries may be transformed into refugees as rising seas overtake island nations. Everywhere and everyone on Earth will feel the impacts of climate change.

While the situation might seem grim, there is still hope. There are many individuals, movements, and organizations working to reduce greenhouse gas emissions, limit climate change, and help communities adapt to its effects. Change must occur at every level—including international agreements, national policies, community-centered changes, and even individual efforts.

Still, scientific models have shown that we can't afford to drag our feet. The time to act is now, and there is much work to be done. But it's possible to look at the climate crisis as an opportunity. People around the world can come together and create more resilient communities, greener and more just policies, and a healthier, more sustainable world.

How You Can Help

There's a place in the movement for anyone who would like to create a safer and healthier world. Here are some actions you can take:

- Raise money to donate to organizations that raise awareness about climate change and promote climate change solutions. You can donate to any of the organizations discussed in previous chapters, and there are many more!
- Volunteer with a local organization or your local government to help make your community more environmentally friendly and more resilient to climate change.
- Raise awareness about climate change and the impacts it will have on the world and on your community.
- Write letters to your local, state, and national lawmakers to express your concern about climate change. Tell them about any actions you'd like to see them support.

You can make an impact by volunteering with local groups dedicated to fighting climate change.

GLOSSARY

atoll: a coral island consisting of a reef surrounding a lagoon

basin: land that has been drained of water by a river and its branches

carbon sink: a location (such as the ocean, the soil, or a forest) that stores substances which contain carbon and especially carbon dioxide

coral bleaching: when corals expel the algae that live in their tissues, causing them to turn white. Corals are bright and colorful because of these microscopic algae. When the coral experiences stress, the algae leave, causing the coral to fade and appear bleached.

crop yield: a measurement of the amount of agricultural production harvested per unit of land area

cyclone: a storm or system of winds that rotates around a center of low atmospheric pressure, advances at a speed of 20 to 30 miles (32 to 48 km) an hour, and often brings heavy rain

delta: wetlands that form when rivers empty their water and sediment into another body of water, such as an ocean, lake, or another river

desertification: the process of becoming desert (as from land mismanagement or climate change)

drought: a period of dryness, especially when prolonged

greenhouse gas: any of various gaseous compounds (such as carbon dioxide or methane) that absorb infrared radiation, trap heat in the atmosphere, and contribute to the greenhouse effect

hydroelectric power: electricity produced from generators driven by turbines that convert the potential energy of falling or fast-flowing water into electricity

Indigenous: of or relating to the earliest known inhabitants of a place and especially of a place that was colonized by a now-dominant group

irrigation: the supply of water to land and crops

monsoon: the season of the southwest monsoon in India and adjacent areas that is characterized by very heavy rainfall

ocean acidification: when the absorption of carbon dioxide (CO_2) from the atmosphere makes the ocean more acidic over an extended period of time

outburst flood: a sudden release of a significant amount of water retained in a glacial lake

ozone: a gas with a strong odor that is a major air pollutant in the lower atmosphere of Earth but is helpful in the upper atmosphere

paleoclimatologist: a person who studies paleoclimatology, which is the study of past climates

particulate matter: a mixture of solid particles and liquid droplets found in the air. Some particles, such as dust, dirt, soot, or smoke, are large or dark enough to be seen with the naked eye.

polar vortex: a large area of low pressure and cold air surrounding both of Earth's poles. It always exists near the poles but weakens in summer and strengthens in winter. The term *vortex* refers to the counterclockwise flow of air that helps keep the colder air near the poles.

positive feedback loop: a process in which some initial change causes some secondary change that, in turn, increases the effects of the initial change

precipitation: water or the amount of water that falls to the earth as hail, mist, rain, sleet, or snow

resilient: characterized or marked by the ability to recover from or adjust to misfortune or change

sustainable: of, relating to, or being a method of harvesting or using a resource so that the resource is not depleted or permanently damaged

SOURCE NOTES

4 "one of the . . . floodings ever seen": "Millions in Bangladesh impacted by one of the worst floodings ever seen," International Federation of Red Cross and Red Crescent Societies, June 28, 2022, https://www.ifrc.org/press-release/millions-bangladesh-impacted-one-worst-floodings-ever-seen.

8 "climate change is . . . and global climates": "What is Climate Change?" NASA, accessed April 4, 2024, https://science.nasa.gov/climate-change/what-is-climate-change/.

14 "Nine of the . . . occurred since 1996.": "Climate Change Indicators: Weather and Climate," United States Environmental Protection Agency, July 26, 2023, https://.epa.gov/climate-indicators/weather-climate.

13 "a world beyond fossil fuels": 350.org, accessed August 11, 2024, https://350.org/.

26 "promote and expand pesticide resistance": Ma, Chun-Sen, Wei Zhang, Yu Peng, Fei Zhao, Xiang-Qian Chang, Kun Xing, Liang Zhu, Gang Ma, He-ping Yang, and Volker H. W. Rudolf, "Climate Warming Promotes Pesticide Resistance through Expanding the Overwintering Range of a Global Pest," *Nature Communications* 12, no. 5351, September 2021, https://doi.org/10.1038/s41467-021-25505-7.

32 "it is unlawful . . . the climate crisis." Lyons, Kate, "Climate Refugees Can't Be Returned Home, Says Landmark UN Human Rights Ruling," *Guardian*, January 20, 2020, https://www.theguardian.com/world/2020/jan/20/climate-refugees-cant-be-returned-home-says-landmark-un-human-rights-ruling.

35 "between 2030 and . . . heat stress alone.": "Climate Change," World Health Organization, October 12, 2023, https://www.who.int/news-room/fact-sheets/detail/climate-change-and-health.

SELECTED BIBLIOGRAPHY

Barba, Amanda. "Kiribati: The First Country the Ocean Will Claim." Journal of Diplomacy and International Relations, June 15, 2021. https://blogs.shu.edu/journalofdiplomacy/2021/06/kiribati-the-first-country-the-ocean-will-claim/.

Chandrasekhar, Vaishnavi. "As Himalayan Glaciers Melt, a Water Crisis Looms in South Asia." Yale Environment 360, October 3, 2022. https://e360.yale.edu/features/himalayas-glaciers-climate-change.

Davies, Bethan. "The World's Mountain 'Water Towers' Are Melting, Putting 1.9 Billion People at Risk." Conversation, December 17, 2019. https://theconversation.com/the-worlds-mountain-water-towers-are-melting-putting-1-9-billion-people-at-risk-128501.

Gray, Ellen. "Global Climate Change Impact on Crops Expected Within 10 Years, NASA Study Finds." NASA, November 21, 2021. https://climate.nasa.gov/news/3124/global-climate-change-impact-on-crops-expected-within-10-years-nasa-study-finds/.

Hausfather, Zeke. "Explainer: What Climate Models Tell Us About Future Rainfall." Carbon Brief, January 19, 2018. https://www.carbonbrief.org/explainer-what-climate-models-tell-us-about-future-rainfall/.

Jahan, Sam. "Third of Bangladesh Underwater as Monsoon Drenches Region." Phys.org, July 14, 2020. https://phys.org/news/2020-07-bangladesh-underwater-monsoon-drenches-region.html.

Kan-Rice, Pamela. "Climate Change to Drive Surge in Insects That Attack Almonds, Peaches, Walnuts." USDA National Institute of Food and Agriculture, December 11, 2023. https://www.nifa.usda.gov/about-nifa/impacts/climate-change-drive-surge-insects-attack-almonds-peaches-walnuts.

"Launch of an Atlas on the Retreat of Andean Glaciers and the Reduction of Glacial Waters." UNESCO. Updated April 20, 2023. https://www.unesco.org/en/articles/launch-atlas-retreat-andean-glaciers-and-reduction-glacial-waters.

Lyons, Kate. "Climate Refugees Can't Be Returned Home, Says Landmark UN Human Rights Ruling." *Guardian*, January 20, 2020. https://www.theguardian.com/world/2020/jan/20/climate-refugees-cant-be-returned-home-says-landmark-un-human-rights-ruling.

FURTHER INFORMATION

BOOKS

Andra, Kayla. *Climate Change Basics: What Is Happening To Our World*. Minneapolis: Twenty-First Century Books, 2026.
This informative resource introduces the core concepts of climate change. From greenhouse gases to global warming, *Climate Change Basics* has it covered.

Gerry, Lisa. *Water! Why Every Drop Counts and How You Can Start Making Waves to Protect It*. Washington, DC: National Geographic Kids, 2023.
In this book, you'll learn why water is so important and how demand for it is increasing worldwide. Learn all about water issues, and more importantly, how you can help save water.

Harman, Alice. *Climate Change and How We'll Fix It: The Real Problem and What We Can Do to Fix It*. New York: Union Square Kids, 2021.
This guide enlightens young people about why climate change is real, why it's serious, what's causing it, and how to fix it. It explains why many adults aren't doing enough, why one group of people alone can't solve it, and what the roadblocks are.

Hirsch, Rebecca E. *Where Have All the Birds Gone?* Minneapolis: Twenty-First Century Books, 2022.
Birds play an important role in ecosystems. This book dives deep into the important roles birds play in the environment and human communities, why their populations are declining, and how climate change affects them. Above all, find out how you can help these animals.

Kehoe, Rachel. *Improving Farming and Food Science to Fight Climate Change*. Lake Elmo, MN: Focus Readers, 2023.
This book delves into how farming and food production contribute to climate change. Learn about the challenges scientists are facing and discover how we can improve agriculture so that it can help solve the climate crisis instead.

WEBSITES

Climate Kids: Resources

https://www.climatekids.org/resources

Climate Kids has a wealth of cool resources about climate change, such as the Climate Kids Activity Book and an online educational portal where you can learn more about many of the topics introduced to you in this book. Climate Kids even sponsors a Youth Climate Challenge if you'd like to take action.

Earth.Org Kids

https://kids.earth.org/

Explore news articles about the environment written especially for young people. If you're a writer or an artist yourself, you can even submit a story or artwork to the website on their submission page.

Global Ice Viewer

https://climate.nasa.gov/interactives/global-ice-viewer/

Made by NASA, this Global Ice Viewer interactive takes you on a virtual tour of glaciers around the world. See pictures of the glaciers from the past and learn about how much they're melting. You can also learn about the satellites that scientists use to measure how much glaciers are melting.

Illuminate

https://ic3uwaterlooca.itch.io/illuminate

Developed by the Waterloo Climate Institute, Illuminate is an online interactive game where players explore solutions to climate change effects. The game consists of two missions: reducing greenhouse gas emissions and preparing coastal, rural, and urban communities for the impacts they'll experience.

Kids' Guide to Coral Reef Conservation

https://coral.org/en/blog/kids-guide-to-coral-reef-conservation/

Coral.org has put together a "Kids' Guide to Coral Reef Conservation." Through their website, you can also join the Alliance of Kid Conservationists.

INDEX

ABOUT THE AUTHOR

Rebecca Schroeder is a writer and science teacher living in the South Carolina low country. She studied Physics & Astronomy and Environmental Studies at the University of Pittsburgh, grounding her work in both scientific inquiry and environmental advocacy. As a dual M.A. in International Affairs and Natural Resources & Sustainable Development from American University and the UN-Mandated University for Peace in Costa Rica, Rebecca brings a global perspective to her writing. In her free time, she enjoys hiking, traveling, and stargazing.

PHOTO ACKNOWLEDGMENTS

Paulo M. F. Pires/Shutterstock, cover; zakir1346/Shutterstock, p. 5; Mongkolchon Akesin/Shutterstock, p. 6; Florian Nimsdorf/Shutterstock, p. 8; AnnaRoth 108, p. 10; Dima Berlin/Shutterstock, p. 13; Indi_kator, p. 15; Abbi Warnock-Matthews/Shutterstock, p. 18; Clickontheway/ Shutterstock, p. 21; William Edge/Shutterstock, p. 23; Natalliaskn/ Shutterstock. p. 25; Edwin Muller Photography/Shutterstock, p. 28; SennaRelax/Shutterstock, p. 30; maloff/Shutterstock, p. 33; Towering Goals/Shutterstock, p. 36; Alex Lerner/Shutterstock, p. 39; boulham/ Shutterstock, p. 42; John Holmdahl/Shutterstock, p. 44; Vlad 61/ Shutterstock, p. 46; Becca in Colorado/Shutterstock, p. 47; Marco Taliano de Marcio/Shutterstock, p. 49; Ivan Ventura/Shutterstock, p. 51; ArieStudio/Shutterstock, p. 53; DC Studio/Shutterstock, p. 55.